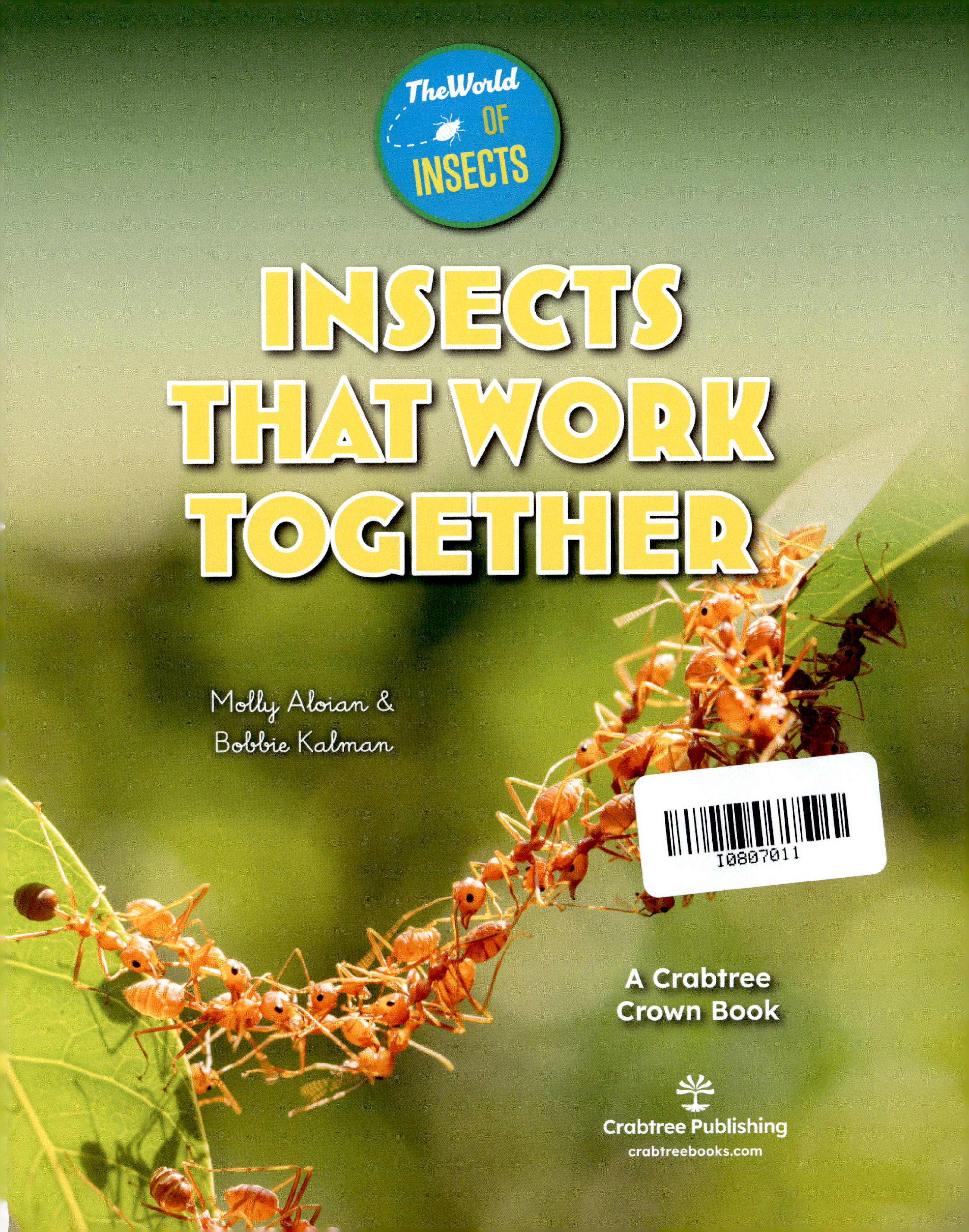

The World OF INSECTS

INSECTS THAT WORK TOGETHER

Molly Aloian &
Bobbie Kalman

A Crabtree Crown Book

Crabtree Publishing
crabtreebooks.com

INSECTS THAT WORK TOGETHER

Editor-in-Chief Bobbie Kalman

Writing team Molly Aloian, Bobbie Kalman

Editors Kathryn Smithyman, Kelley MacAulay, Reagan Miller, Rebecca Sjonger

Consultant Patricia Loesche, Ph.D., Animal Behavior Program, Department of Psychology, University of Washington

Design and photo research Katherine Kantor

Cover design Rhea Magaro-Wallace

Production manager Candice Campbell

Images Shutterstock; Margaret Amy Salter: p. 31

Crabtree Publishing

crabtreebooks.com 800-387-7650

In Canada: We acknowledge the financial support of the Government of Canada through the Canada Book Fund for our publishing activities.

Printed in the U.S.A./CP022026

Published in Canada
Crabtree Publishing
616 Welland Ave.
St. Catharines, Ontario
L2M 5V6

Published in the United States
Crabtree Publishing
347 Fifth Ave
Suite 1402-145
New York, NY 10016

Library and Archives Canada Cataloguing in Publication
Available at the Library and Archives Canada

Library of Congress Cataloging-in-Publication Data
Available at the Library of Congress

Hardcover: 978-1-0398-7311-7
Paperback: 978-1-0398-7369-8
Ebook (pdf): 978-1-0398-7419-0
Epub: 978-1-0398-7468-8

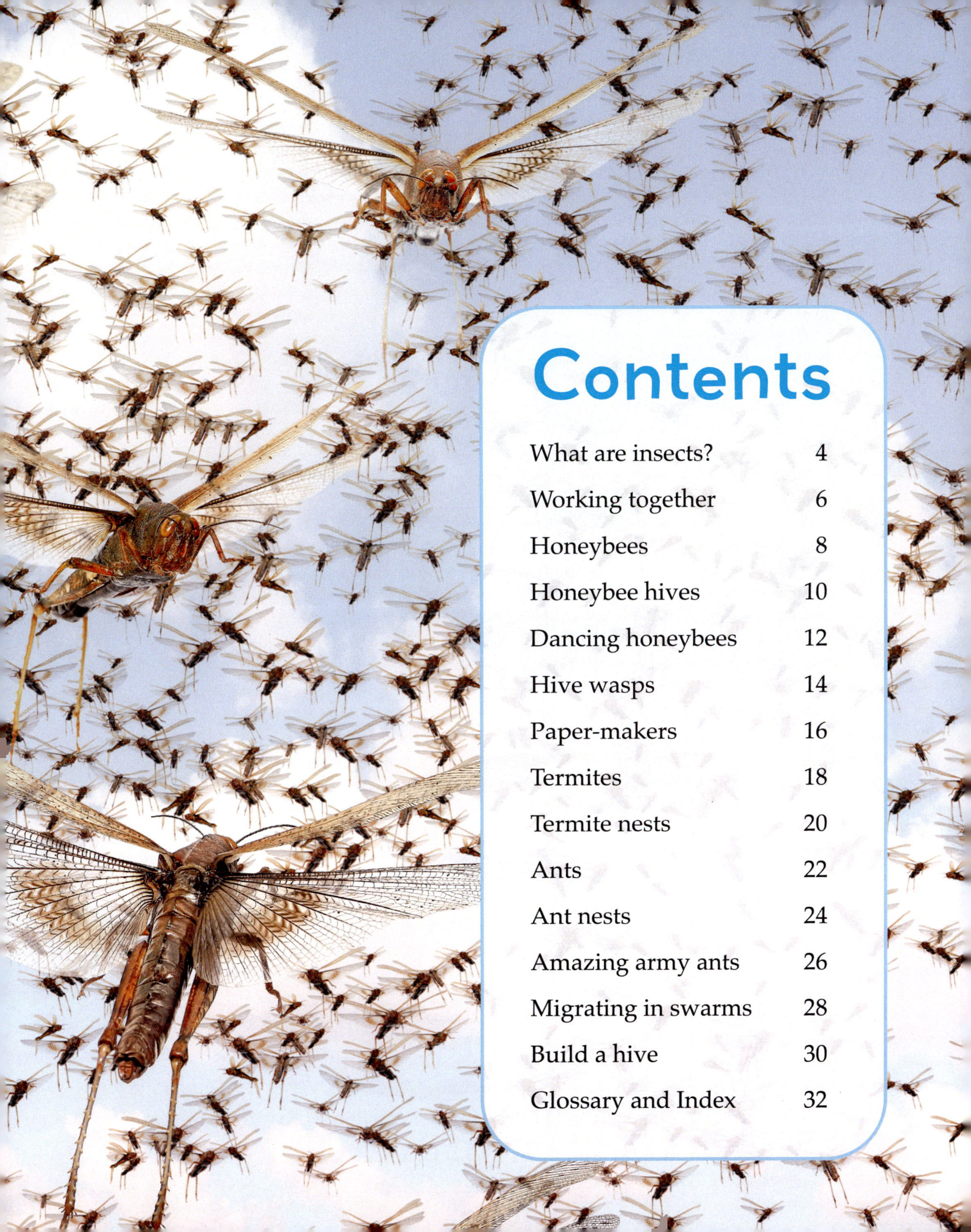

Contents

What are insects?

Insects are animals. All insects are **invertebrates**. Invertebrates are animals with no **backbones**. A backbone is a group of bones in the middle of an animal's back.

Instead of backbones, insects have hard outer coverings called **exoskeletons**. An exoskeleton covers and protects an insect's whole body, including the insect's legs and head.

Body parts

An insect's body has three main parts—a head, a **thorax**, and an **abdomen**. An insect's eyes and **mouthparts** are on its head. There are also two feelers called **antennae** on an insect's head. An insect's legs and wings are attached to its thorax. All insects have six legs.

Did you know?

Many insects have wings, but some insects have no wings. Insects that have wings can fly from place to place. Some insects have two pairs of wings, but others have only one pair.

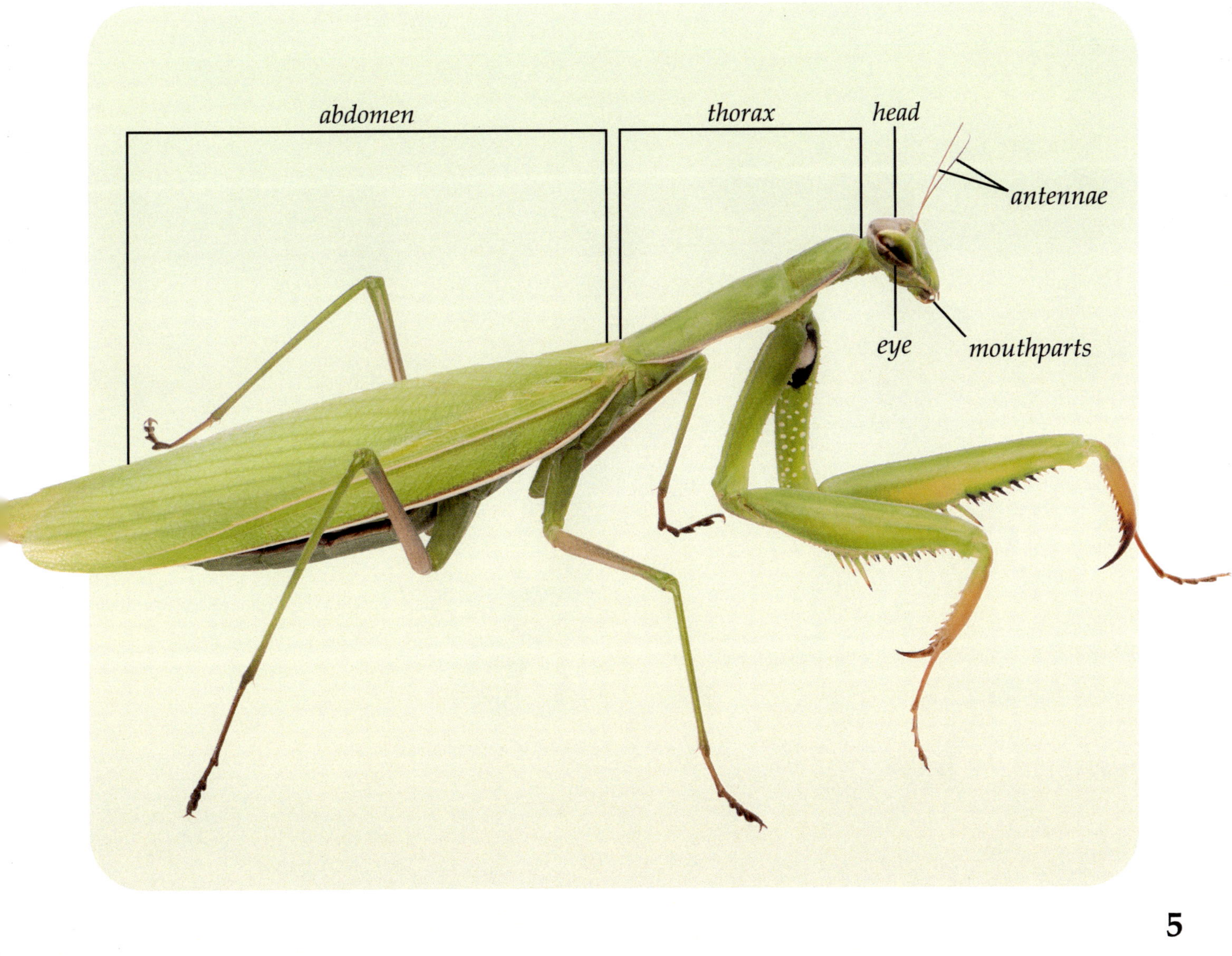

Working together

Some insects live and work together. Insects that live together form a big group called a **colony**. A colony can contain more than one million insects! Insects that live in colonies are often called **social insects**.

Honeybees, termites, ants, and hive wasps are social insects. Social insects work together to find food, to build homes, and to raise **larvae** or **nymphs**. Larvae and nymphs are two kinds of young insects.

Safety in numbers

Social insects have better chances of staying alive because they work together. They work as a team to keep all the insects in the colony safe and healthy. Social insects gather food and share it with one another. Most social insects also build homes, called **nests**, where the colonies live.

*Most of the insects in a colony are **workers**. Workers are the insects that do most of the work. They work both inside and outside of the nest.*

Honeybees

Honeybees are social insects that form colonies. The colonies live and work together in nests called **hives**. Each honeybee colony is made up of thousands of honeybees. There are three kinds of honeybees in a colony. They are workers, **drones**, and a **queen**. Each honeybee colony often has only one queen.

Workers are the smallest honeybees. All workers are females.

Drones are male honeybees. Drones are bigger than workers.

The queen is the largest honeybee. She is a female.

Did you know?
Honeybee larvae hatch from eggs. Larvae do not have eyes, legs, wings, or antennae, but they do have mouthparts. They use their mouthparts to eat. Larvae eat a lot!

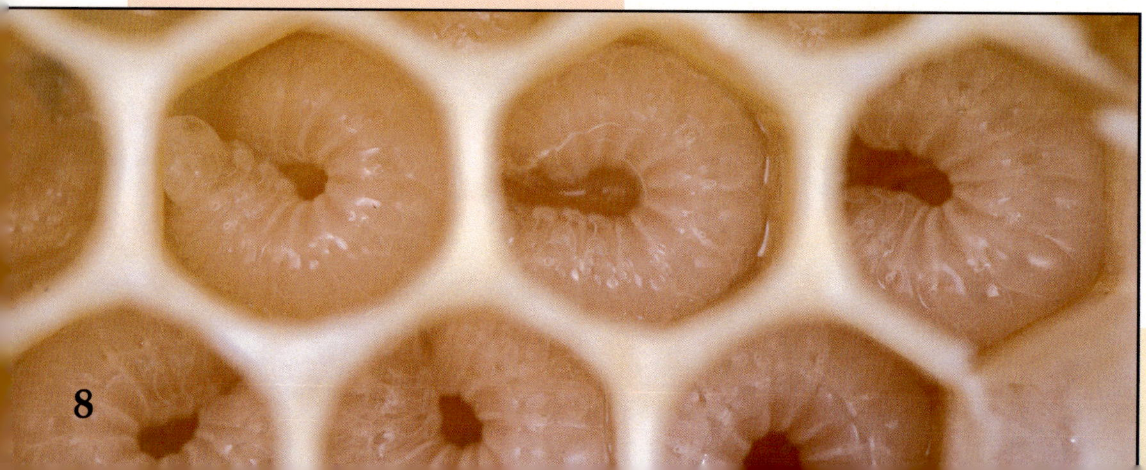

In a few weeks, these honeybee larvae will have eyes, legs, wings, and antennae.

Workers

Workers have many jobs in the hive. They build the hive, keep it clean, and protect it from other insects. Workers also take care of the larvae as they grow.

Drones

Drones do not work as much as worker honeybees do. Drones have only one job. They **mate**, or join together, with the queen honeybee so she can lay eggs.

The queen

The queen honeybee also has only one job. She lays eggs inside the hive. A larva hatches from each egg.

Workers leave the hive to collect ***pollen*** *and* ***nectar*** *from flowers. Workers use pollen and nectar to make food for all the other honeybees.*

The queen lays up to 1,500 eggs each day!

egg

Honeybee hives

Worker honeybees work together to make a hive. They make the hive from **beeswax**. Beeswax is a substance that workers make in their bodies. The wax comes out of their bodies in flakes. Worker bees use their mouthparts and front legs to soften and shape the flakes of wax. They shape the wax into small units called **cells**. There are about 100,000 cells in one honeybee hive.

All the cells in a hive have six sides. Having six sides makes the cells very strong.

Heated hives

Wax is softer and easier to shape in a warm hive. To keep the hive warm, the worker honeybees **beat**, or flap, their wings as they work. The moving bodies of the workers create heat and warm up the hive.

Did you know?

The cells in a hive are built side by side and back to back, so that no space is wasted between them. Honeybees use the cells for storing food and raising larvae.

The cell at the top of the picture holds a larva.

Dancing honeybees

A colony of honeybees must **communicate**, or send messages to one another. Honeybees communicate to make sure all the work in the hive gets done. Honeybees communicate in different ways. One way they communicate is by touching and smelling one another with their antennae. Honeybees also communicate by flying in certain ways.

Round and round

When a worker honeybee finds a source of food such as nectar, it returns to the hive to let the other workers know where the food is. If nectar is close to the hive, the worker does a **round dance**.

round dance

Wanna waggle?

When nectar is far away from the hive, a worker honeybee flies in a different way. It does a **waggle dance**. The waggle dance tells the other worker honeybees how far away the nectar is. It also tells them the direction in which the nectar can be found.

The waggle is the zigzag in the middle.

Hive wasps

Hornets, yellow jackets, and paper wasps are three types of hive wasps. Hive wasps live in colonies. Wasp colonies can contain thousands of wasps. Like a honeybee colony, a wasp colony is made up of three different types of wasps—workers, drones, and a queen.

hornet

wasp

yellow jacket

Working wasps

Some of the jobs of wasp workers, drones, and queens are the same as the jobs of honeybee workers, drones, and queens. Worker wasps are all female. They build and care for the nest, gather food, and raise the larvae. Drone wasps mate with the queen. The queen wasp lays eggs.

Did you know?

Like honeybees, wasps communicate with one another. Wasps send messages to other wasps by giving off **scents**, or smells. For example, wasps release certain scents to warn other wasps of danger.

These adult worker wasps are caring for the larvae inside the nest. The workers feed the larvae and keep them clean.

Paper-makers

Hive wasps live together in hives. Some hive wasps build underground hives. Others build hives that hang from trees. The workers build the hives and keep them clean and safe.

Pulp to paper

Wasps make their hives out of paperlike materials. When making a hive, workers use their mouthparts to chew up small pieces of wood. They mix the wood with their **saliva** to make a soft, moist substance called **pulp**. Workers then use their front legs and mouthparts to form the pulp into cells. The pulp looks like paper when it dries.

This wasp hive is hanging from a branch.

Did you know?

Different workers do different jobs. Some workers leave the hive to catch other insects. They bring the insects back to the hive to feed to the larvae. Other workers leave the hive and bring back pieces of wood. The wood is used to fix holes in the hive. Another group of workers stays inside the hive. This group keeps the hive clean and protects it from other animals.

This wasp is putting paper caps over the cells that hold larvae. The caps help protect the larvae as they grow into adults. When the larvae are finished growing, they push through the caps.

Termites

Most termite colonies are made up of three types of termites—**reproductives**, workers, and **soldiers**. Reproductives are termites that are able to **reproduce**, or make babies.

Queens and kings

A termite colony has one queen. She is a female reproductive. The colony also has a male reproductive. He is known as the king.

Mating and laying eggs

The king termite's job is to mate with the queen. The queen's job is to lay thousands of eggs. When the eggs hatch, the nymphs grow up to be reproductives, workers, or soldiers.

king termite

The queen termite, shown above, is the biggest termite in the colony. Her large abdomen is filled with eggs.

Workers

Worker termites find food for the whole colony. They build and repair the nest. They also care for nymphs. In a termite colony, the workers are both male and female, but workers cannot reproduce with one another.

Soldiers

Soldier termites, shown above, protect the colony. Soldiers often have large, sharp mouthparts. They use their mouthparts to attack intruders such as ants.

Termite nests

A colony of termites works as a team to build a nest. The termites make tunnels and **chambers**, or rooms, inside the nest. They build their nests inside trees or in wooden buildings. Some make their nests in the soil. Underground nests often include huge piles of soil and sand, which are called **mounds**.

Dampwood termites, shown above, often live inside damp, rotting wood.

Drywood termites live in wooden poles, wooden buildings, or in dead, dry trees.

Eating through

To build nests in trees or wooden buildings, worker termites chew and eat through the wood. The workers make tunnels and chambers as they eat. The king and queen termites live in one of these chambers. It is called the **royal chamber.**

Gathering and gluing

Other types of termites have workers that gather pieces of wood, soil, or sand. They bring these materials back to the nest. The workers glue the materials together with their saliva. They use the materials to form the walls of the tunnels and the chambers.

Some mounds are 30 feet (9 m) tall. You can see how huge this mound is when you compare its size to the size of the woman in front of it!

Some ants work only inside the colony. Others leave the colony to find food.

Ants

Ant colonies are usually made up of workers, males, and queens. Certain ant colonies have more than one queen, however. Other colonies do not have a queen at all.

Jobs for workers

Most of the ants in a colony are workers. All worker ants are females. Worker ants build and clean the nest, gather food, and care for the larvae. Some types of ants have workers that are soldier ants. Like the soldiers in termite colonies, the soldiers in ant colonies have large mouthparts. They use their mouthparts to fight off attackers.

Workers clean and care for the eggs that the queen lays.

Tiny but strong

Ants are tiny, but they are strong. In fact, ants are strong enough to carry or drag leaves or other insects. The leaves or insects often weigh up to 20 times as much as an ant weighs! The leafcutter ants shown below are carrying big pieces of leaves. They are using their mouthparts to carry the leaves.

Did you know?

Queen ants live a lot longer than worker ants live. Some queens live for ten to twenty years! Workers only live for two to six months.

These ants are working together to make a nest in the thorns of a thorn acacia tree.

Ant nests

Some ants make dirt mounds at the entrances of their nests. Some ants make big dirt mounds. The mounds can be up to six feet (2 m) high!

Different types of ants live in different types of nests. Some make nests in rotting wood. Others make nests out of leaves or inside the thorns of certain trees. Many ants make nests in soil.

A soil nest

When making a soil nest, workers use their feet and mouthparts to dig through the soil and make tunnels. Other workers carry pieces of soil up to the surface of the ground to form a mound.

Did you know?

Weaver ants, shown on this page, make nests out of leaves. A group of workers pulls the edges of two leaves together. A different group of workers carries larvae back and forth across the edges of the leaves. The larvae make a strong, sticky substance called **silk** in their bodies. The silk glues the edges of the leaves together.

Adult weaver ants do not make silk in their bodies. Weaver ants cannot make their nests without the silk from larvae.

These weaver ants are looking for leaves that they can use to build their nest. When their nest is finished, it will look like a ball of leaves.

Amazing army ants

Most ants make **permanent** nests, but army ants do not. Army ants are almost always moving from place to place! Workers carry the eggs and the larvae as the colony moves. When army ants need to rest, they make a **temporary** nest. The colony uses this nest for a short time, before the ants are on the move again!

Did you know?

Army ants make a temporary nest by clinging to one another and forming a tight ball with their bodies. They keep the queen, the eggs, and the larvae deep inside the nest, where they are safe.

*A colony of army ants travels in a **swarm**. A swarm is a large group of moving insects.*

On the move

Army ants work together to kill **prey**. As they move from place to place, they bite and sting any animals in their path. By working together, the ants make sure that there is enough food for the colony to eat. A colony of army ants can eat thousands of insects in one day! They can also kill and eat bigger animals, such as lizards, snakes, and birds.

These army ants are eating the larvae inside a wasp nest.

Migrating in swarms

Locusts and monarch butterflies are not social insects, but they sometimes gather together to **migrate**. To migrate is to travel from one place to another for a certain amount of time. Locusts and monarchs migrate in huge swarms. By migrating in swarms, these insects have better chances of staying alive during their long journeys.

Migrating monarchs

Monarchs that live in North America migrate because they cannot survive cold winter weather. Before winter begins, most monarchs fly in swarms to Mexico or to California, where the weather is warm.

*These migrating monarch butterflies have stopped to rest high up among the leaves on a tree, where they are safe from **predators**.*

*A swarm often contains millions of locusts. The locusts eat a lot of plants as they migrate. They often eat **crops**. Crops are plants that people grow for food.*

A lot of locusts

Locusts migrate when their **population** grows too large. Population is the total number of animals living in a certain area. When the population of locusts is too big, there are not enough plants for all the locusts in that area to eat. The locusts must migrate to new areas, where there is more food.

Build a hive

How many sides are there on the cells of honeybee hives? The cells are **hexagons**. Hexagons are shapes that have six sides. Learn how to make a honeybee hive by following the instructions on these pages.

Trace the hexagon shown here onto five pieces of paper. Make sure you trace the circle and the lines outside the hexagon, as well.

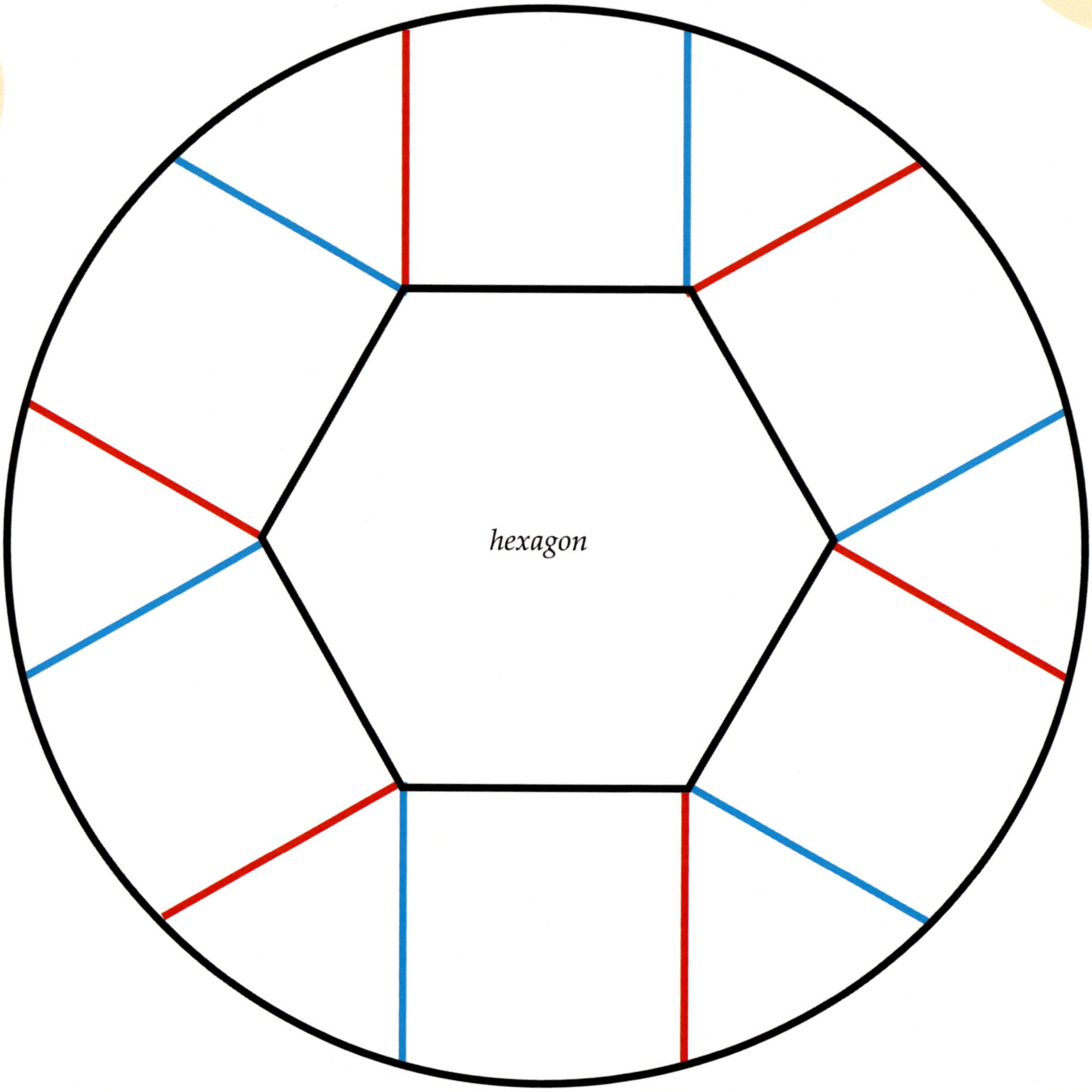

Using a pair of scissors, cut out the circle and along the red lines. Fold the paper on the edges of the blue lines. Now, fold all six sides of the hexagon toward the center of the paper.

After you have made all the folds, tape down the folded flaps. You have made a cell for your hive! Follow the same steps with the other four pieces of paper.

When you have finished all five cells, paint your cells yellow to look as if they are made of beeswax. Glue the cells together to make a hive. Use the pictures in this book to help you draw pictures of honeybees to put inside your hive.

Glossary

Note: Boldfaced words that are defined in the text may not appear in the glossary.

cell A small enclosed space

mouthparts The parts on an insect's head that are used to grip and eat food

nectar A sweet liquid found in flowers

permanent Describing something that lasts for or is used for a long time

pollen A powdery substance that plants make

predator An animal that hunts and eats other animals

prey Animals that are hunted and eaten by other animals

saliva A clear liquid found in an animal's mouth

silk A strong, thin, sticky fiber that certain insect larvae are able to make inside their bodies

temporary Describing something that lasts for or is used for a short time

Index